Super Handy Planner

CW00529979

Phone Number

Calendar D

Weekly Plan

Bonuses

Website Passwords Log

Personal Goals

Vacation Planning

Packing List

Party Planning

Christmas Day Planner

Grocery List

Notebook

Lined Pages

Notes

Grid Dots

Love this Design?

@MariaLeonaDesign

Important Info

FAMILY NAME: _____

ADDRESS: _____

HOME PHONE: _____

IN AN EMERGENCY CALL:

PARENT 1

NAME: _____

WORK PHONE: _____

CELL PHONE: _____

PARENT 2

NAME: _____

WORK PHONE: _____

CELL PHONE: _____

CHILDREN'S NAMES

_____

_____

_____

CHILDREN'S CELL PHONE NUMBERS

_____

_____

_____

SCHOOL NAME(S)

_____

_____

_____

SCHOOL PHONE NUMBERS

_____

_____

_____

EXTENDED FAMILY

_____

_____

_____

_____

NEIGHBORS & FRIENDS

_____

_____

_____

_____

NOTES:

Phone Numbers - eMails

FAMILY

FRIENDS

FREQUENT PLAYDATES

NEIGHBORS

BABYSITTERS

SCHOOLS/DAYCARE

KIDS' AFTER-SCHOOL PROGRAMS

KIDS' FAVORITE ATTRACTIONS

SALONS

GYMS/CLUBS

RESTAURANTS

TAKE-OUT/DELIVERY

VET

GROOMER

Phone Numbers - eMails

CONTRACTORS

HANDYMAN

REPAIRS

CLEANING SERVICES

LAWN SERVICE

SNOW REMOVAL

GARBAGE PICKUP

RECYCLING PICKUP

DECORATOR

OTHER

NOTES:

Phone Numbers - eMails

CONTRACTORS

HANDYMAN

REPAIRS

CLEANING SERVICES

LAWN SERVICE

SNOW REMOVAL

GARBAGE PICKUP

RECYCLING PICKUP

DECORATOR

OTHER

NOTES:

January

Monthly Focus

1 _____
2 _____
3 _____

Special Dates

____ _____
____ _____
____ _____
____ _____
____ _____

Home Keeping Tasks

- _____
- _____
- _____
- _____
- _____
- _____
- _____

Goals for the Month

_____ ☐
_____ ☐
_____ ☐
_____ ☐
_____ ☐
_____ ☐

_____ ☐
_____ ☐
_____ ☐
_____ ☐
_____ ☐
_____ ☐

_____ ☐
_____ ☐
_____ ☐
_____ ☐
_____ ☐
_____ ☐

Notes

February

Monthly Focus

Top Three Things

1 _____
2 _____
3 _____

Special Dates

___ _____
___ _____
___ _____
___ _____
___ _____

Home Keeping Tasks

☐ _____
☐ _____
☐ _____
☐ _____
☐ _____
☐ _____
☐ _____

Goals for the Month

☐ _____
☐ _____
☐ _____
☐ _____
☐ _____
☐ _____

☐ _____
☐ _____
☐ _____
☐ _____
☐ _____
☐ _____

☐ _____
☐ _____
☐ _____
☐ _____
☐ _____
☐ _____

Notes

_____
_____
_____
_____
_____
_____
_____
_____
_____
_____
_____
_____
_____
_____
_____
_____
_____
_____
_____
_____
_____
_____
_____

March

Monthly Focus

1 _____
2 _____
3 _____

Special Dates

____ _____
____ _____
____ _____
____ _____
____ _____

Home Keeping Tasks

☐ _____
☐ _____
☐ _____
☐ _____
☐ _____
☐ _____
☐ _____

Goals for the Month

☐ _____
☐ _____
☐ _____
☐ _____
☐ _____
☐ _____

☐ _____
☐ _____
☐ _____
☐ _____
☐ _____
☐ _____

☐ _____
☐ _____
☐ _____
☐ _____
☐ _____
☐ _____

Notes

April

Monthly Focus

Top Three Things

1 _____
2 _____
3 _____

Special Dates

____ _____
____ _____
____ _____
____ _____
____ _____

Home Keeping Tasks

☐ _____
☐ _____
☐ _____
☐ _____
☐ _____
☐ _____
☐ _____

Goals for the Month

_____ ☐
_____ ☐
_____ ☐
_____ ☐
_____ ☐
_____ ☐

_____ ☐
_____ ☐
_____ ☐
_____ ☐
_____ ☐
_____ ☐

_____ ☐
_____ ☐
_____ ☐
_____ ☐
_____ ☐
_____ ☐

Notes

_____
_____
_____
_____
_____
_____
_____
_____
_____
_____
_____
_____
_____
_____
_____
_____
_____
_____
_____
_____
_____
_____
_____
_____

May

Monthly Focus

1 _____
2 _____
3 _____

Special Dates

_____ _____
_____ _____
_____ _____
_____ _____
_____ _____

Home Keeping Tasks

☐ _____
☐ _____
☐ _____
☐ _____
☐ _____
☐ _____
☐ _____

Goals for the Month

_____ ☐
_____ ☐
_____ ☐
_____ ☐
_____ ☐
_____ ☐

_____ ☐
_____ ☐
_____ ☐
_____ ☐
_____ ☐
_____ ☐

_____ ☐
_____ ☐
_____ ☐
_____ ☐
_____ ☐
_____ ☐

Notes
_____
_____
_____
_____
_____
_____
_____
_____
_____
_____
_____
_____
_____
_____
_____
_____
_____
_____
_____
_____
_____
_____
_____
_____
_____
_____
_____
_____
_____

June

Monthly Focus

Top Three Things

1. _____
2. _____
3. _____

Special Dates

_____ _____
_____ _____
_____ _____
_____ _____
_____ _____

Home Keeping Tasks

- [ ] _____
- [ ] _____
- [ ] _____
- [ ] _____
- [ ] _____
- [ ] _____
- [ ] _____

Goals for the Month

- [ ] _____
- [ ] _____
- [ ] _____
- [ ] _____
- [ ] _____
- [ ] _____

- [ ] _____
- [ ] _____
- [ ] _____
- [ ] _____
- [ ] _____
- [ ] _____

- [ ] _____
- [ ] _____
- [ ] _____
- [ ] _____
- [ ] _____
- [ ] _____

Notes

July

Monthly Focus

Top Three Things

1 _____
2 _____
3 _____

Special Dates

_____ _____
_____ _____
_____ _____
_____ _____
_____ _____

Home Keeping Tasks

☐ _____
☐ _____
☐ _____
☐ _____
☐ _____
☐ _____
☐ _____

Goals for the Month

_____ ☐
_____ ☐
_____ ☐
_____ ☐
_____ ☐
_____ ☐

_____ ☐
_____ ☐
_____ ☐
_____ ☐
_____ ☐
_____ ☐

_____ ☐
_____ ☐
_____ ☐
_____ ☐
_____ ☐
_____ ☐

Notes

August

nthly Focus

Top Three Things

1 _____
2 _____
3 _____

Special Dates

— _____
— _____
— _____
— _____
— _____

Is for the Month

Home Keeping Tasks

☐ _____
☐ _____
☐ _____
☐ _____
☐ _____
☐ _____
☐ _____

☐ _____
☐ _____
☐ _____
☐ _____
☐ _____
☐ _____

☐
☐
☐
☐
☐
☐

☐
☐
☐
☐
☐
☐

Notes

September

Monthly Focus

Top Three Things

1 _____
2 _____
3 _____

Special Dates

_____ _____
_____ _____
_____ _____
_____ _____
_____ _____

Home Keeping Tasks

☐ _____
☐ _____
☐ _____
☐ _____
☐ _____
☐ _____
☐ _____

Goals for the Month

_____ ☐
_____ ☐
_____ ☐
_____ ☐
_____ ☐
_____ ☐

_____ ☐
_____ ☐
_____ ☐
_____ ☐
_____ ☐
_____ ☐

_____ ☐
_____ ☐
_____ ☐
_____ ☐
_____ ☐
_____ ☐

Notes

_____
_____
_____
_____
_____
_____
_____
_____
_____
_____
_____
_____
_____
_____
_____
_____
_____
_____
_____
_____
_____
_____
_____
_____
_____
_____

October

Monthly Focus

1 _____
2 _____
3 _____

Special Dates

_____ _____
_____ _____
_____ _____
_____ _____
_____ _____

Home Keeping Tasks
☐ _____
☐ _____
☐ _____
☐ _____
☐ _____
☐ _____
☐ _____

Goals for the Month

_____ ☐
_____ ☐
_____ ☐
_____ ☐
_____ ☐
_____ ☐

_____ ☐
_____ ☐
_____ ☐
_____ ☐
_____ ☐
_____ ☐

_____ ☐
_____ ☐
_____ ☐
_____ ☐
_____ ☐
_____ ☐

Notes

November

Monthly Focus

Top Three Things
1 _____
2 _____
3 _____

_____ _____
_____ _____
_____ _____
_____ _____
_____ _____

Home Keeping Tasks
☐ _____
☐ _____
☐ _____
☐ _____
☐ _____
☐ _____
☐ _____

Goals for the Month

_____ ☐
_____ ☐
_____ ☐
_____ ☐
_____ ☐
_____ ☐

_____ ☐
_____ ☐
_____ ☐
_____ ☐
_____ ☐
_____ ☐

_____ ☐
_____ ☐
_____ ☐
_____ ☐
_____ ☐
_____ ☐

Notes
_____
_____
_____
_____
_____
_____
_____
_____
_____
_____
_____
_____
_____
_____
_____
_____
_____
_____
_____
_____
_____
_____
_____
_____
_____

December

Monthly Focus

1 _____
2 _____
3 _____

Special Dates

_____
_____
_____
_____
_____

Home Keeping Tasks

- [ ] _____
- [ ] _____
- [ ] _____
- [ ] _____
- [ ] _____
- [ ] _____
- [ ] _____

Goals for the Month

- [ ] _____
- [ ] _____
- [ ] _____
- [ ] _____
- [ ] _____
- [ ] _____

- [ ] _____
- [ ] _____
- [ ] _____
- [ ] _____
- [ ] _____
- [ ] _____

- [ ] _____
- [ ] _____
- [ ] _____
- [ ] _____
- [ ] _____
- [ ] _____

Notes

Week 1

Monday

Tuesday

Wednesday

Thursday

Friday

Saturday

Sunday

Places to Go

- ○
- ○
- ○
- ○
- ○
- ○

People to See

- ○
- ○
- ○
- ○
- ○

Things to Do

- ○
- ○
- ○
- ○
- ○
- ○
- ○
- ○
- ○
- ○
- ○

Special Reminders

- ○
- ○
- ○
- ○
- ○
- ○

Week 2

Monday

Tuesday

Wednesday

Thursday

Friday

Saturday

Sunday

Places to Go
-
-
-
-
-
-

People to See
-
-
-
-
-
-

Things to Do
-
-
-
-
-
-
-
-
-
-
-
-

Special Reminders
-
-
-
-
-
-

Week 3

Monday

Tuesday

Wednesday

Thursday

Friday

Saturday

Sunday

Places to Go

- ◯
- ◯
- ◯
- ◯
- ◯
- ◯

People to See

- ◯
- ◯
- ◯
- ◯
- ◯
- ◯

Things to Do

- ◯
- ◯
- ◯
- ◯
- ◯
- ◯
- ◯
- ◯
- ◯
- ◯
- ◯
- ◯

Special Reminders

- ◯
- ◯
- ◯
- ◯
- ◯
- ◯

Week 4

Monday

Tuesday

Wednesday

Thursday

Friday

Saturday

Sunday

Places to Go

- ○
- ○
- ○
- ○
- ○
- ○

People to See

- ○
- ○
- ○
- ○
- ○
- ○

Things to Do

- ○
- ○
- ○
- ○
- ○
- ○
- ○
- ○
- ○
- ○
- ○

Special Reminders

- ○
- ○
- ○
- ○
- ○
- ○

Week 5

Monday

Tuesday

Wednesday

Thursday

Friday

Saturday

Sunday

People to See

Things to Do

Special Reminders

Week 6

Monday

Tuesday

Wednesday

Thursday

Friday

Saturday

Sunday

Places to Go

People to See

Things to Do

Special Reminders

Week 7

Monday

Tuesday

Wednesday

Thursday

Friday

Saturday

Sunday

Places to Go

- ○
- ○
- ○
- ○
- ○
- ○

People to See

- ○
- ○
- ○
- ○
- ○
- ○

Things to Do

- ○
- ○
- ○
- ○
- ○
- ○
- ○
- ○
- ○
- ○
- ○
- ○

Special Reminders

- ○
- ○
- ○
- ○
- ○
- ○

Week 8

onday

esday

ednesday

ursday

day

turday

nday

Places to Go

- ○
- ○
- ○
- ○
- ○
- ○

People to See

- ○
- ○
- ○
- ○
- ○
- ○

Things to Do

- ○
- ○
- ○
- ○
- ○
- ○
- ○
- ○
- ○
- ○
- ○
- ○
- ○

Special Reminders

- ○
- ○
- ○
- ○
- ○
- ○

Week 8

Monday

Tuesday

Wednesday

Thursday

Friday

Saturday

Sunday

Places to Go

- ○
- ○
- ○
- ○
- ○
- ○

People to See

- ○
- ○
- ○
- ○
- ○
- ○

Things to Do

- ○
- ○
- ○
- ○
- ○
- ○
- ○
- ○
- ○
- ○
- ○
- ○
- ○

Special Reminders

- ○
- ○
- ○
- ○
- ○
- ○
- ○

Week 9

Monday

Tuesday

Wednesday

Thursday

Friday

Saturday

Sunday

Places to Go

○
○
○
○
○
○

People to See

○
○
○
○
○
○

Things to Do

○
○
○
○
○
○
○
○
○
○
○
○

Special Reminders

○
○
○
○
○
○

Week 10

Monday

Tuesday

Wednesday

Thursday

Friday

Saturday

Sunday

People to See

Things to Do

Special Reminders

Week 11

Monday

Tuesday

Wednesday

Thursday

Friday

Saturday

Sunday

Places to Go

- ○
- ○
- ○
- ○
- ○
- ○

People to See

- ○
- ○
- ○
- ○
- ○
- ○

Things to Do

- ○
- ○
- ○
- ○
- ○
- ○
- ○
- ○
- ○
- ○
- ○
- ○

Special Reminders

- ○
- ○
- ○
- ○
- ○
- ○

Week 12

Monday

Tuesday

Wednesday

Thursday

Friday

Saturday

Sunday

Places to Go

People to See

Things to Do

Special Reminders

Week 13

nday

esday

dnesday

ırsday

day

urday

ıday

Places to Go

- ○
- ○
- ○
- ○
- ○
- ○

People to See

- ○
- ○
- ○
- ○
- ○
- ○

Things to Do

- ○
- ○
- ○
- ○
- ○
- ○
- ○
- ○
- ○
- ○
- ○
- ○
- ○

Special Reminders

- ○
- ○
- ○
- ○
- ○
- ○

Week 14

Monday

Tuesday

Wednesday

Thursday

Friday

Saturday

Sunday

Places to Go

- ○
- ○
- ○
- ○
- ○
- ○

People to See

- ○
- ○
- ○
- ○
- ○
- ○

Things to Do

- ○
- ○
- ○
- ○
- ○
- ○
- ○
- ○
- ○
- ○
- ○
- ○
- ○

Special Reminders

- ○
- ○
- ○
- ○
- ○
- ○

Week 15

Monday

Tuesday

Wednesday

Thursday

Friday

Saturday

Sunday

Places to Go

- ○
- ○
- ○
- ○
- ○
- ○

People to See

- ○
- ○
- ○
- ○
- ○
- ○

Things to Do

- ○
- ○
- ○
- ○
- ○
- ○
- ○
- ○
- ○
- ○
- ○
- ○

Special Reminders

- ○
- ○
- ○
- ○
- ○
- ○

Week 16

Monday

Tuesday

Wednesday

Thursday

Friday

Saturday

Sunday

Week 17

Monday

Tuesday

Wednesday

Thursday

Friday

Saturday

Sunday

Places to Go

- ◯
- ◯
- ◯
- ◯
- ◯
- ◯

People to See

- ◯
- ◯
- ◯
- ◯
- ◯
- ◯

Things to Do

- ◯
- ◯
- ◯
- ◯
- ◯
- ◯
- ◯
- ◯
- ◯
- ◯
- ◯
- ◯

Special Reminders

- ◯
- ◯
- ◯
- ◯
- ◯
- ◯
- ◯

Week 18

Monday

Tuesday

Wednesday

Thursday

Friday

Saturday

Sunday

Places to Go

People to See

Things to Do

Special Reminders

Week 19

nday

esday

dnesday

rsday

ay

urday

day

Places to Go

- ○
- ○
- ○
- ○
- ○
- ○

People to See

- ○
- ○
- ○
- ○
- ○

Things to Do

- ○
- ○
- ○
- ○
- ○
- ○
- ○
- ○
- ○
- ○
- ○
- ○

Special Reminders

- ○
- ○
- ○
- ○
- ○
- ○

Week 20

Monday

Tuesday

Wednesday

Thursday

Friday

Saturday

Sunday

Places to Go

- ○
- ○
- ○
- ○
- ○
- ○

People to See

- ○
- ○
- ○
- ○
- ○

Things to Do

- ○
- ○
- ○
- ○
- ○
- ○
- ○
- ○
- ○
- ○
- ○

Special Reminders

- ○
- ○
- ○
- ○
- ○
- ○

Week 21

Monday

Tuesday

Wednesday

Thursday

Friday

Saturday

Sunday

Places to Go

People to See

Things to Do

Special Reminders

Week 22

Monday

Tuesday

Wednesday

Thursday

Friday

Saturday

Sunday

Places to Go

People to See

Things to Do

Special Reminders

Week 23

Monday

Tuesday

Wednesday

Thursday

Friday

Saturday

Sunday

Places to Go

○
○
○
○
○
○

People to See

○
○
○
○
○
○

Things to Do

○
○
○
○
○
○
○
○
○
○
○
○

Special Reminders

○
○
○
○
○
○

Week 24

Monday

Tuesday

Wednesday

Thursday

Friday

Saturday

Sunday

Places to Go

- ◯
- ◯
- ◯
- ◯
- ◯
- ◯

People to See

- ◯
- ◯
- ◯
- ◯
- ◯
- ◯

Things to Do

- ◯
- ◯
- ◯
- ◯
- ◯
- ◯
- ◯
- ◯
- ◯
- ◯
- ◯
- ◯

Special Reminders

- ◯
- ◯
- ◯
- ◯
- ◯
- ◯

Week 25

nday

sday

dnesday

rsday

lay

rday

day

Places to Go

○
○
○
○
○
○
○

People to See

○
○
○
○
○
○

Things to Do

○
○
○
○
○
○
○
○
○
○
○
○
○

Special Reminders

○
○
○
○
○
○
○

Week 26

Monday

Tuesday

Wednesday

Thursday

Friday

Saturday

Sunday

Places to Go

People to See

Things to Do

Special Reminders

Week 27

Monday

Tuesday

Wednesday

Thursday

Friday

Saturday

Sunday

Places to Go

-
-
-
-
-
-

People to See

-
-
-
-
-
-

Things to Do

-
-
-
-
-
-
-
-
-
-
-
-

Special Reminders

-
-
-
-
-
-

Week 28

Monday

Tuesday

Wednesday

Thursday

Friday

Saturday

Sunday

Places to Go

○
○
○
○
○
○

People to See

○
○
○
○
○

Things to Do

○
○
○
○
○
○
○
○
○
○
○
○
○

Special Reminders

○
○
○
○
○
○

Week 29

Monday

Tuesday

Wednesday

Thursday

Friday

Saturday

Sunday

Places to Go

-
-
-
-
-
-
-

People to See

-
-
-
-
-
-

Things to Do

-
-
-
-
-
-
-
-
-
-
-
-
-

Special Reminders

-
-
-
-
-
-

Week 30

Monday

Tuesday

Wednesday

Thursday

Friday

Saturday

Sunday

Places to Go

-
-
-
-
-
-
-

People to See

-
-
-
-
-
-

Things to Do

-
-
-
-
-
-
-
-
-
-
-
-

Special Reminders

-
-
-
-
-
-

Week 31

nday

esday

dnesday

irsday

lay

urday

iday

Week 32

Monday

Tuesday

Wednesday

Thursday

Friday

Saturday

Sunday

Week 33

Monday

Tuesday

Wednesday

Thursday

Friday

Saturday

Sunday

Places to Go
- ◯
- ◯
- ◯
- ◯
- ◯
- ◯

People to See
- ◯
- ◯
- ◯
- ◯
- ◯
- ◯

Things to Do
- ◯
- ◯
- ◯
- ◯
- ◯
- ◯
- ◯
- ◯
- ◯
- ◯
- ◯
- ◯

Special Reminders
- ◯
- ◯
- ◯
- ◯
- ◯
- ◯

Week 34

Monday

Tuesday

Wednesday

Thursday

Friday

Saturday

Sunday

Places to Go

People to See

Things to Do

Special Reminders

Week 35

Monday

Tuesday

Wednesday

Thursday

Friday

Saturday

Sunday

Places to Go
- ◯
- ◯
- ◯
- ◯
- ◯
- ◯

People to See
- ◯
- ◯
- ◯
- ◯
- ◯
- ◯

Things to Do
- ◯
- ◯
- ◯
- ◯
- ◯
- ◯
- ◯
- ◯
- ◯
- ◯
- ◯
- ◯

Special Reminders
- ◯
- ◯
- ◯
- ◯
- ◯
- ◯

Week 36

Monday

Tuesday

Wednesday

Thursday

Friday

Saturday

Sunday

Places to Go

People to See

Things to Do

Special Reminders

Week 37

nday

sday

dnesday

ursday

lay

urday

day

Places to Go

- ◯
- ◯
- ◯
- ◯
- ◯
- ◯

People to See

- ◯
- ◯
- ◯
- ◯
- ◯

Things to Do

- ◯
- ◯
- ◯
- ◯
- ◯
- ◯
- ◯
- ◯
- ◯
- ◯
- ◯

Special Reminders

- ◯
- ◯
- ◯
- ◯
- ◯
- ◯

Week 38

Monday

Tuesday

Wednesday

Thursday

Friday

Saturday

Sunday

Places to Go

People to See

Things to Do

Special Reminders

Week 39

Monday

Tuesday

Wednesday

Thursday

Friday

Saturday

Sunday

Places to Go

- ○
- ○
- ○
- ○
- ○
- ○

People to See

- ○
- ○
- ○
- ○
- ○
- ○

Things to Do

- ○
- ○
- ○
- ○
- ○
- ○
- ○
- ○
- ○
- ○
- ○
- ○

Special Reminders

- ○
- ○
- ○
- ○
- ○
- ○

Week 40

Monday

Tuesday

Wednesday

Thursday

Friday

Saturday

Sunday

Places to Go

People to See

Things to Do

Special Reminders

Week 41

onday

esday

ednesday

ursday

iday

turday

nday

Week 42

Monday

Tuesday

Wednesday

Thursday

Friday

Saturday

Sunday

Places to Go

- ○
- ○
- ○
- ○
- ○
- ○

People to See

- ○
- ○
- ○
- ○
- ○

Things to Do

- ○
- ○
- ○
- ○
- ○
- ○
- ○
- ○
- ○
- ○
- ○
- ○

Special Reminders

- ○
- ○
- ○
- ○
- ○
- ○

Week 43

Monday

Tuesday

Wednesday

Thursday

Friday

Saturday

Sunday

Places to Go

- ○
- ○
- ○
- ○
- ○
- ○

People to See

- ○
- ○
- ○
- ○
- ○
- ○

Things to Do

- ○
- ○
- ○
- ○
- ○
- ○
- ○
- ○
- ○
- ○
- ○

Special Reminders

- ○
- ○
- ○
- ○
- ○
- ○

Week 44

Monday

Tuesday

Wednesday

Thursday

Friday

Saturday

Sunday

Places to Go

-
-
-
-
-
-

People to See

-
-
-
-
-
-

Things to Do

-
-
-
-
-
-
-
-
-
-
-
-

Special Reminders

-
-
-
-
-
-

Week 45

Monday

Tuesday

Wednesday

Thursday

Friday

Saturday

Sunday

Places to Go

- ○
- ○
- ○
- ○
- ○
- ○

People to See

- ○
- ○
- ○
- ○
- ○
- ○

Things to Do

- ○
- ○
- ○
- ○
- ○
- ○
- ○
- ○
- ○
- ○
- ○
- ○

Special Reminders

- ○
- ○
- ○
- ○
- ○
- ○
- ○

Week 46

Monday

Tuesday

Wednesday

Thursday

Friday

Saturday

Sunday

Places to Go

○
○
○
○
○
○

People to See

○
○
○
○
○

Things to Do

○
○
○
○
○
○
○
○
○
○
○
○

Special Reminders

○
○
○
○
○
○

Week 47

onday

esday

ednesday

ursday

iday

turday

nday

Places to Go

○
○
○
○
○
○

People to See

○
○
○
○
○
○

Things to Do

○
○
○
○
○
○
○
○
○
○
○
○

Special Reminders

○
○
○
○
○
○

Week 48

Monday

Tuesday

Wednesday

Thursday

Friday

Saturday

Sunday

Places to Go

- ○
- ○
- ○
- ○
- ○
- ○

People to See

- ○
- ○
- ○
- ○
- ○
- ○

Things to Do

- ○
- ○
- ○
- ○
- ○
- ○
- ○
- ○
- ○
- ○
- ○
- ○

Special Reminders

- ○
- ○
- ○
- ○
- ○
- ○

Week 49

nday

esday

dnesday

ırsday

lay

urday

ıday

Places to Go
- ○
- ○
- ○
- ○
- ○
- ○

People to See
- ○
- ○
- ○
- ○
- ○

Things to Do
- ○
- ○
- ○
- ○
- ○
- ○
- ○
- ○
- ○
- ○
- ○

Special Reminders
- ○
- ○
- ○
- ○
- ○
- ○

Week 50

Monday

Tuesday

Wednesday

Thursday

Friday

Saturday

Sunday

Places to Go

People to See

Things to Do

Special Reminders

Week 51

Monday

Tuesday

Wednesday

Thursday

Friday

Saturday

Sunday

Places to Go

People to See

Things to Do

Special Reminders

Week 52

Monday

Tuesday

Wednesday

Thursday

Friday

Saturday

Sunday

Places to Go

○
○
○
○
○
○

People to See

○
○
○
○
○

Things to Do

○
○
○
○
○
○
○
○
○
○
○
○

Special Reminders

○
○
○
○
○
○

Week 53

onday

esday

ednesday

ursday

iday

turday

nday

Places to Go

- ○
- ○
- ○
- ○
- ○
- ○

People to See

- ○
- ○
- ○
- ○
- ○
- ○

Things to Do

- ○
- ○
- ○
- ○
- ○
- ○
- ○
- ○
- ○
- ○
- ○
- ○
- ○
- ○

Special Reminders

- ○
- ○
- ○
- ○
- ○
- ○

My Personal Goals

This format will help you clarify your long-term goals. Be specific when listing goals, include at least 3 actions needed in order to achieve your goals, and don't forget a due date to ensure you take action. Keep this list in a place where you will see it each day; it will really help you stay focused on what's most important to you!

MY GOALS	ACTION STEPS	DUE DATE
LONG TERM	1.	
	2.	
	3.	
	1.	
	2.	
	3.	
SHORT TERM	1.	
	2.	
	3.	
	1.	
	2.	
	3.	
NOW	1.	
	2.	
	3.	
	1.	
	2.	
	3.	

My Personal Goals

This format will help you clarify your long-term goals. Be specific when listing goals, include at least 3 actions needed in order to achieve your goals, and don't forget a due date to ensure you take action. Keep this list in a place where you will see it each day; it will really help you stay focused on what's most important to you!

MY GOALS	ACTION STEPS	DUE DATE
LONG TERM		
	1.	
	2.	
	3.	
	1.	
	2.	
	3.	
SHORT TERM		
	1.	
	2.	
	3.	
	1.	
	2.	
	3.	
NOW		
	1.	
	2.	
	3.	
	1.	
	2.	
	3.	

Vacation Planning

DATES:

LOCATION:

BUDGET:

GETTING THERE

CAR RENTAL

LODGING

WHAT TO PACK

RECOMMENDED SIGHTS/RESTAURANTS

ITINERARY

NOTES:

Packing List

THE ESSENTIALS

- ○ Tickets
- ○ Passports
- ○ Car Rental Info
- ○ Itinerary
- ○ Reservation Info
- ○ Cell Phone Charger
- ○ Car Cell Phone Charger
- ○ Foreign Currency
- ○ Wallet/Purse
- ○ Medications

CLOTHING

- ○ Undergarments/Socks
- ○ Shirts/Blouses
- ○ Jeans/Pants/Shorts
- ○ Sweaters
- ○ Dresses/Skirts
- ○ Jacket
- ○ Pajamas/Robe/Slippers
- ○ Shoes/Sneakers
- ○ Workout Clothing
- ○

TOILETRIES

- ○ Shampoo/Conditioner
- ○ Cleansers/Soap
- ○ Toothbrush/Toothpaste/Floss
- ○ Cosmetics
- ○ Deodorant
- ○ Lip Balm
- ○ Brush/Comb
- ○ Razor/Shaving Cream
- ○ Contact Lens Solution

MISCELLANEOUS

- ○ Jewelry/Watch
- ○ Hairdryer
- ○ Camera/Video Camera
- ○ Memory Cards
- ○ Glasses/Sunglasses
- ○ Travel Guidebooks
- ○ Travel Journal
- ○ Books/Magazines
- ○ First Aid Kit
- ○ Antibacterial Wipes/Lotion
- ○ Stain Removal Wipes

FOR THE KIDS

- ○ Stroller
- ○ Diapers/Wipes/Changing
- ○ Pad
- ○ Diaper Bag
- ○ Food/Formula
- ○ Bottles
- ○ Sippy Cups
- ○ Utensils
- ○ Bibs
- ○ Medicines
- ○ Toys/Games
- ○ Stuffed Animal
- ○ Blanket
- ○ Books
- ○ Activity Books
- ○ Handheld Games
- ○
- ○
- ○
- ○

SKI ESSENTIALS

- ○ Waterproof Ski Jacket/Pants
- ○ Long Underwear
- ○ Skis/Boots/Poles
- ○ Ski Helmet
- ○ Goggles
- ○ Ski Gloves
- ○ Neck Warmer
- ○ Hat/Headband
- ○ Ski Socks
- ○ Hand/Foot Warmers
- ○ Turtlenecks/Extra Sweaters
- ○ Snow Boots
- ○ Ski Bag

BEACH ESSENTIALS

- ○ Swimsuit/Cover Up
- ○ Sunscreen/After-Sun Lotion
- ○ Beach Towels
- ○ Beach Chairs
- ○ Beach Umbrella
- ○ Goggles
- ○ Beach/Pool Toys
- ○ Sunhat
- ○ Sandals
- ○ Beach Bag

OTHER

- ○
- ○
- ○
- ○
- ○

Websites & Passwords

WEBSITE	USERNAME	PASSWORD

Websites & Passwords

WEBSITE	USERNAME	PASSWORD

Websites & Passwords

WEBSITE	USERNAME	PASSWORD

Websites & Passwords

WEBSITE	USERNAME	PASSWORD

Notes

Notes

Notes

Notes

Notes

Notes

Notes

Party Planning

DETAILS:

MENU

BEVERAGES

GUEST NAME

RSVP Y/N

Party Planning

DETAILS:

MENU

BEVERAGES

GUEST NAME

RSVP Y/N

Party Planning

DETAILS:

MENU

BEVERAGES

GUEST NAME

RSVP Y/N

Party Planning

DETAILS:

MENU

BEVERAGES

GUEST NAME

RSVP Y/N

Christmas Day Planner

GUEST NAME	# OF ADULTS	# OF KIDS	FOOD ITEM TO BRING

TOTAL # OF GUESTS _____

GROCERIES

APPETIZERS: _____

ENTREES: _____

SIDES: _____

DESSERTS: _____

BEVERAGES: _____

Grocery List

FRUITS
Apples
Bananas
Oranges
Lemons
Berries
Grapes
Melons

VEGETABLES
Lettuce
Spinach
Carrots
Onions
Garlic
Tomatoes
Cucumbers
Squash
Potatoes
Broccoli

MEAT
Beef
Chicken
Turkey
Fish
Seafood
Pork
Sausage
Hot Dogs
Hamburgers
Cold Cuts

DAIRY
Milk
Juice
Cheese
Butter
Eggs
Tortillas
Yogurt
Whipped Cream

PACKAGED
Chips
Cookies
Crackers
Popcorn
Pretzels
Nuts
Candy
Dips/Salsa
Fruit Cups
Energy Bars

BREADS
White
Wheat
Fresh Baked
Bagels
Muffins
English Muffins
Pita
Rolls
Donuts/Pastries

GRAINS
Pasta
Rice
Couscous
Dried Beans
Stuffing
Bread Crumbs

BREAKFAST FOOD
Oatmeal
Pancake Mix
Granola
Cereal Bars
Syrup
Cereals

BAKING GOODS
Baking Mixes
Flours
Sugars

CANNED
Soup
Broth
Tomatoes
Pasta Sauce
Beans
Tuna
Fruits
Vegetables

BEVERAGES
Soda
Beer/Wine
Energy Drinks
Juice
Water

MISCELLANEOUS
Ketchup
Mayonnaise
Salad Dressing
Peanut Butter
Jelly
Coffee
Tea
Oils
Vinegar
Salt
Pepper
Spices

FROZEN
Ice Cream
Waffles
Pizza
Fries
Bread
Meals
Snacks
Juice
Vegetables

HOUSEHOLD GOODS
Cleaning Products
Dish Liquid
Hand Soap
All-purpose
Bathroom
Floor/Carpet
Wood/Furniture
Glass/Window
Sponges
Trash Bags
Air Freshener
Hand Sanitizer
Miscellaneous

LAUNDRY
Detergent
Fabric Softener
Bleach
Starch
Stain Remover

PAPER PRODUCTS
Napkins
Paper Towels
Facial Tissue
Bathroom Tissue
Paper Plates
Paper Cups

MISC. HOUSEHOLD
Lunch Bags
Storage Bags
Storage Containers
Batteries
Coffee Filters

OTHER

Grocery List

RUITS
ples
nanas
ranges
mons
rries
apes
elons

EGETABLES
ttuce
inach
rrots
nions
arlic
matoes
ucumbers
uash
tatoes
occoli

EAT
ef
icken
rkey
h
afood
rk
usage
t Dogs
amburgers
ld Cuts

AIRY
lk
ce
eese
tter
gs
rtillas
gurt
hipped Cream

PACKAGED
Chips
Cookies
Crackers
Popcorn
Pretzels
Nuts
Candy
Dips/Salsa
Fruit Cups
Energy Bars

BREADS
White
Wheat
Fresh Baked
Bagels
Muffins
English Muffins
Pita
Rolls
Donuts/Pastries

GRAINS
Pasta
Rice
Couscous
Dried Beans
Stuffing
Bread Crumbs

BREAKFAST FOOD
Oatmeal
Pancake Mix
Granola
Cereal Bars
Syrup
Cereals

BAKING GOODS
Baking Mixes
Flours
Sugars

CANNED
Soup
Broth
Tomatoes
Pasta Sauce
Beans
Tuna
Fruits
Vegetables

BEVERAGES
Soda
Beer/Wine
Energy Drinks
Juice
Water

MISCELLANEOUS
Ketchup
Mayonnaise
Salad Dressing
Peanut Butter
Jelly
Coffee
Tea
Oils
Vinegar
Salt
Pepper
Spices

FROZEN
Ice Cream
Waffles
Pizza
Fries
Bread
Meals
Snacks
Juice
Vegetables

HOUSEHOLD GOODS
Cleaning Products
Dish Liquid
Hand Soap
All-purpose
Bathroom
Floor/Carpet
Wood/Furniture
Glass/Window
Sponges
Trash Bags
Air Freshener
Hand Sanitizer
Miscellaneous

LAUNDRY
Detergent
Fabric Softener
Bleach
Starch
Stain Remover

PAPER PRODUCTS
Napkins
Paper Towels
Facial Tissue
Bathroom Tissue
Paper Plates
Paper Cups

MISC. HOUSEHOLD
Lunch Bags
Storage Bags
Storage Containers
Batteries
Coffee Filters

OTHER

Grocery List

FRUITS
Apples
Bananas
Oranges
Lemons
Berries
Grapes
Melons

VEGETABLES
Lettuce
Spinach
Carrots
Onions
Garlic
Tomatoes
Cucumbers
Squash
Potatoes
Broccoli

MEAT
Beef
Chicken
Turkey
Fish
Seafood
Pork
Sausage
Hot Dogs
Hamburgers
Cold Cuts

DAIRY
Milk
Juice
Cheese
Butter
Eggs
Tortillas
Yogurt
Whipped Cream

PACKAGED
Chips
Cookies
Crackers
Popcorn
Pretzels
Nuts
Candy
Dips/Salsa
Fruit Cups
Energy Bars

BREADS
White
Wheat
Fresh Baked
Bagels
Muffins
English Muffins
Pita
Rolls
Donuts/Pastries

GRAINS
Pasta
Rice
Couscous
Dried Beans
Stuffing
Bread Crumbs

BREAKFAST FOOD
Oatmeal
Pancake Mix
Granola
Cereal Bars
Syrup
Cereals

BAKING GOODS
Baking Mixes
Flours
Sugars

CANNED
Soup
Broth
Tomatoes
Pasta Sauce
Beans
Tuna
Fruits
Vegetables

BEVERAGES
Soda
Beer/Wine
Energy Drinks
Juice
Water

MISCELLANEOUS
Ketchup
Mayonnaise
Salad Dressing
Peanut Butter
Jelly
Coffee
Tea
Oils
Vinegar
Salt
Pepper
Spices

FROZEN
Ice Cream
Waffles
Pizza
Fries
Bread
Meals
Snacks
Juice
Vegetables

HOUSEHOLD GOODS
Cleaning Products
Dish Liquid
Hand Soap
All-purpose
Bathroom
Floor/Carpet
Wood/Furniture
Glass/Window
Sponges
Trash Bags
Air Freshener
Hand Sanitizer
Miscellaneous

LAUNDRY
Detergent
Fabric Softener
Bleach
Starch
Stain Remover

PAPER PRODUCTS
Napkins
Paper Towels
Facial Tissue
Bathroom Tissue
Paper Plates
Paper Cups

MISC. HOUSEHOLD
Lunch Bags
Storage Bags
Storage Containers
Batteries
Coffee Filters

OTHER

Grocery List

JITS
les
nas
nges
ons
ies
oes
ons

GETABLES
uce
ach
ots
ons
lic
atoes
umbers
ash
toes
ccoli

AT
f
cken
key

ood

sage
Dogs
nburgers
d Cuts

IRY

e
ese
ter
s
tillas
urt
ipped Cream

PACKAGED
Chips
Cookies
Crackers
Popcorn
Pretzels
Nuts
Candy
Dips/Salsa
Fruit Cups
Energy Bars

BREADS
White
Wheat
Fresh Baked
Bagels
Muffins
English Muffins
Pita
Rolls
Donuts/Pastries

GRAINS
Pasta
Rice
Couscous
Dried Beans
Stuffing
Bread Crumbs

BREAKFAST FOOD
Oatmeal
Pancake Mix
Granola
Cereal Bars
Syrup
Cereals

BAKING GOODS
Baking Mixes
Flours
Sugars

CANNED
Soup
Broth
Tomatoes
Pasta Sauce
Beans
Tuna
Fruits
Vegetables

BEVERAGES
Soda
Beer/Wine
Energy Drinks
Juice
Water

MISCELLANEOUS
Ketchup
Mayonnaise
Salad Dressing
Peanut Butter
Jelly
Coffee
Tea
Oils
Vinegar
Salt
Pepper
Spices

FROZEN
Ice Cream
Waffles
Pizza
Fries
Bread
Meals
Snacks
Juice
Vegetables

HOUSEHOLD GOODS
Cleaning Products
Dish Liquid
Hand Soap
All-purpose
Bathroom
Floor/Carpet
Wood/Furniture
Glass/Window
Sponges
Trash Bags
Air Freshener
Hand Sanitizer
Miscellaneous

LAUNDRY
Detergent
Fabric Softener
Bleach
Starch
Stain Remover

PAPER PRODUCTS
Napkins
Paper Towels
Facial Tissue
Bathroom Tissue
Paper Plates
Paper Cups

MISC. HOUSEHOLD
Lunch Bags
Storage Bags
Storage Containers
Batteries
Coffee Filters

OTHER

2020

January
```
Su Mo Tu We Th Fr Sa
          1  2  3  4
 5  6  7  8  9 10 11
12 13 14 15 16 17 18
19 20 21 22 23 24 25
26 27 28 29 30 31
2○ 10○ 17○ 24●
```

February
```
Su Mo Tu We Th Fr Sa
                   1
 2  3  4  5  6  7  8
 9 10 11 12 13 14 15
16 17 18 19 20 21 22
23 24 25 26 27 28 29
1○ 9○ 15○ 23●
```

March
```
Su Mo Tu We Th Fr Sa
 1  2  3  4  5  6  7
 8  9 10 11 12 13 14
15 16 17 18 19 20 21
22 23 24 25 26 27 28
29 30 31
2○ 9○ 16○ 24●
```

April
```
Su Mo Tu We Th Fr Sa
          1  2  3  4
 5  6  7  8  9 10 11
12 13 14 15 16 17 18
19 20 21 22 23 24 25
26 27 28 29 30
1○ 7○ 14○ 22● 30○
```

May
```
Su Mo Tu We Th Fr Sa
                1  2
 3  4  5  6  7  8  9
10 11 12 13 14 15 16
17 18 19 20 21 22 23
24 25 26 27 28 29 30
31
7○ 14○ 22● 29○
```

June
```
Su Mo Tu We Th Fr Sa
    1  2  3  4  5  6
 7  8  9 10 11 12 13
14 15 16 17 18 19 20
21 22 23 24 25 26 27
28 29 30
5○ 13○ 21● 28○
```

July
```
Su Mo Tu We Th Fr Sa
          1  2  3  4
 5  6  7  8  9 10 11
12 13 14 15 16 17 18
19 20 21 22 23 24 25
26 27 28 29 30 31
5○ 12○ 20● 27○
```

August
```
Su Mo Tu We Th Fr Sa
                   1
 2  3  4  5  6  7  8
 9 10 11 12 13 14 15
16 17 18 19 20 21 22
23 24 25 26 27 28 29
30 31
3○ 11○ 18● 25○
```

September
```
Su Mo Tu We Th Fr Sa
       1  2  3  4  5
 6  7  8  9 10 11 12
13 14 15 16 17 18 19
20 21 22 23 24 25 26
27 28 29 30
2○ 10○ 17● 23○
```

October
```
Su Mo Tu We Th Fr Sa
             1  2  3
 4  5  6  7  8  9 10
11 12 13 14 15 16 17
18 19 20 21 22 23 24
25 26 27 28 29 30 31
1○ 9○ 16● 23○ 31○
```

November
```
Su Mo Tu We Th Fr Sa
 1  2  3  4  5  6  7
 8  9 10 11 12 13 14
15 16 17 18 19 20 21
22 23 24 25 26 27 28
29 30
8○ 15● 21○ 30○
```

December
```
Su Mo Tu We Th Fr Sa
       1  2  3  4  5
 6  7  8  9 10 11 12
13 14 15 16 17 18 19
20 21 22 23 24 25 26
27 28 29 30 31
7○ 14● 21○ 29○
```

2021

January
```
Su Mo Tu We Th Fr Sa
                1  2
 3  4  5  6  7  8  9
10 11 12 13 14 15 16
17 18 19 20 21 22 23
24 25 26 27 28 29 30
31
6○ 13● 20○ 28○
```

February
```
Su Mo Tu We Th Fr Sa
    1  2  3  4  5  6
 7  8  9 10 11 12 13
14 15 16 17 18 19 20
21 22 23 24 25 26 27
28
4○ 11● 19○ 27○
```

March
```
Su Mo Tu We Th
 1  2  3  4
 7  8  9 10 11
14 15 16 17 18
21 22 23 24 25
28 29 30 31
5○ 13● 21○ 2
```

April
```
Su Mo Tu We Th Fr Sa
             1  2  3
 4  5  6  7  8  9 10
11 12 13 14 15 16 17
18 19 20 21 22 23 24
25 26 27 28 29 30
4○ 11● 20○ 26○
```

May
```
Su Mo Tu We Th Fr Sa
                   1
 2  3  4  5  6  7  8
 9 10 11 12 13 14 15
16 17 18 19 20 21 22
23 24 25 26 27 28 29
30 31
3○ 11● 19○ 26○
```

June
```
Su Mo Tu We Th
       1  2  3
 6  7  8  9 10
13 14 15 16 17
20 21 22 23
27 28 29 3
2○ 10● 17○ 2
```

July
```
Su Mo Tu We Th Fr Sa
             1  2  3
 4  5  6  7  8  9 10
11 12 13 14 15 16 17
18 19 20 21 22 23 24
25 26 27 28 29 30 31
1● 9○ 17○ 23○ 31○
```

August
```
Su Mo Tu We Th Fr Sa
 1  2  3  4  5  6  7
 8  9 10 11 12 13 14
15 16 17 18 19 20 21
22 23 24 25 26 27 28
29 30 31
8● 15○ 22○ 30○
```

September
```
Su Mo Tu We Th
          1  2
 5  6  7  8  9
12 13 14 15 16
19 20 21 22 23
26 27 28
6● 13○ 20○ 2
```

October
```
Su Mo Tu We Th Fr Sa
                1  2
 3  4  5  6  7  8  9
10 11 12 13 14 15 16
17 18 19 20 21 22 23
24 25 26 27 28 29 30
31
6● 12○ 20○ 28○
```

November
```
Su Mo Tu We Th Fr Sa
    1  2  3  4  5  6
 7  8  9 10 11 12 13
14 15 16 17 18 19 20
21 22 23 24 25 26 27
28 29 30
4● 11○ 19○ 27○
```

December
```
Su Mo Tu We Th
       1  2
 5  6  7  8  9
12 13 14 15 16
19 20 21 22 23
26 27 28 29 3
4● 10○ 18○ 2
```

2022

January
```
Su Mo Tu We Th Fr Sa
                   1
 2  3  4  5  6  7  8
 9 10 11 12 13 14 15
16 17 18 19 20 21 22
23 24 25 26 27 28 29
30 31
2● 9○ 17○ 25○
```

February
```
Su Mo Tu We Th Fr Sa
       1  2  3  4  5
 6  7  8  9 10 11 12
13 14 15 16 17 18 19
20 21 22 23 24 25 26
27 28
1● 8○ 16○ 23○
```

March
```
Su Mo Tu We Th Fr Sa
       1  2  3  4  5
 6  7  8  9 10 11 12
13 14 15 16 17 18 19
20 21 22 23 24 25 26
27 28 29 30 31
2● 10○ 18○ 25○
```

April
```
Su Mo Tu We Th Fr Sa
                1  2
 3  4  5  6  7  8  9
10 11 12 13 14 15 16
17 18 19 20 21 22 23
24 25 26 27 28 29 30
1● 9○ 16○ 23○ 30●
```

May
```
Su Mo Tu We Th Fr Sa
 1  2  3  4  5  6  7
 8  9 10 11 12 13 14
15 16 17 18 19 20 21
22 23 24 25 26 27 28
29 30 31
8○ 16○ 22○ 30●
```

June
```
Su Mo Tu We Th Fr Sa
          1  2  3  4
 5  6  7  8  9 10 11
12 13 14 15 16 17 18
19 20 21 22 23 24 25
26 27 28 29 30
7○ 14○ 20○ 28●
```

July
```
Su Mo Tu We Th Fr Sa
                1  2
 3  4  5  6  7  8  9
10 11 12 13 14 15 16
17 18 19 20 21 22 23
24 25 26 27 28 29 30
31
6○ 13○ 20○ 28●
```

August
```
Su Mo Tu We Th Fr Sa
    1  2  3  4  5  6
 7  8  9 10 11 12 13
14 15 16 17 18 19 20
21 22 23 24 25 26 27
28 29 30 31
5○ 11○ 19○ 27●
```

September
```
Su Mo Tu We Th Fr Sa
             1  2  3
 4  5  6  7  8  9 10
11 12 13 14 15 16 17
18 19 20 21 22 23 24
25 26 27 28 29 30
3○ 10○ 17● 25○
```

October
```
Su Mo Tu We Th Fr Sa
                   1
 2  3  4  5  6  7  8
 9 10 11 12 13 14 15
16 17 18 19 20 21 22
23 24 25 26 27 28 29
30 31
2○ 9○ 17○ 25●
```

November
```
Su Mo Tu We Th Fr Sa
       1  2  3  4  5
 6  7  8  9 10 11 12
13 14 15 16 17 18 19
20 21 22 23 24 25 26
27 28 29 30
1○ 8○ 16○ 23○ 30○
```

December
```
Su Mo Tu We Th Fr Sa
             1  2  3
 4  5  6  7  8  9 10
11 12 13 14 15 16 17
18 19 20 21 22 23 24
25 26 27 28 29 30 31
7○ 16○ 23● 29○
```

2023

January
```
Su Mo Tu We Th Fr Sa
 1  2  3  4  5  6  7
 8  9 10 11 12 13 14
15 16 17 18 19 20 21
22 23 24 25 26 27 28
29 30 31
6○ 14○ 21● 28○
```

February
```
Su Mo Tu We Th Fr Sa
          1  2  3  4
 5  6  7  8  9 10 11
12 13 14 15 16 17 18
19 20 21 22 23 24 25
26 27 28
5○ 13○ 20● 27○
```

March
```
Su Mo Tu We Th F
       1  2
 5  6  7  8  9
12 13 14 15 16 1
19 20 21 22 23 2
26 27 28 29 30 3
7○ 14○ 21● 2
```

April
```
Su Mo Tu We Th Fr Sa
                   1
 2  3  4  5  6  7  8
 9 10 11 12 13 14 15
16 17 18 19 20 21 22
23 24 25 26 27 28 29
30
6○ 13○ 20● 27○
```

May
```
Su Mo Tu We Th Fr Sa
    1  2  3  4  5  6
 7  8  9 10 11 12 13
14 15 16 17 18 19 20
21 22 23 24 25 26 27
28 29 30 31
5○ 12○ 19● 27○
```

June
```
Su Mo Tu We Th F
             1
 4  5  6  7  8
11 12 13 14 15 1
18 19 20 21 22 2
25 26 27 28 29 3
3○ 10○ 18● 2
```

July
```
Su Mo Tu We Th Fr Sa
                   1
 2  3  4  5  6  7  8
 9 10 11 12 13 14 15
16 17 18 19 20 21 22
23 24 25 26 27 28 29
30 31
3○ 9○ 17● 25○
```

August
```
Su Mo Tu We Th Fr Sa
       1  2  3  4  5
 6  7  8  9 10 11 12
13 14 15 16 17 18 19
20 21 22 23 24 25 26
27 28 29 30 31
1○ 8○ 16● 24○ 30○
```

September
```
Su Mo Tu We Th Fr Sa
             1  2
 3  4  5  6  7  8
10 11 12 13 14 1
17 18 19 20 21 2
24 25 26 27 28
6○ 14● 22○ 2
```

October
```
Su Mo Tu We Th Fr Sa
 1  2  3  4  5  6  7
 8  9 10 11 12 13 14
15 16 17 18 19 20 21
22 23 24 25 26 27 28
29 30 31
6○ 14● 21○ 28○
```

November
```
Su Mo Tu We Th Fr Sa
          1  2  3  4
 5  6  7  8  9 10 11
12 13 14 15 16 17 18
19 20 21 22 23 24 25
26 27 28 29 30
5○ 13● 20○ 27○
```

December
```
Su Mo Tu We Th F
             1
 3  4  5  6  7
10 11 12 13 14 1
17 18 19 20 21 2
24 25 26 27 28
31
5○ 12● 19○ 2
```

Printed in Great Britain
by Amazon